Anima
&
The Narrative Limits

Anima
&
The Narrative Limits

Poems

Nabina Das

In this stunning new collection, Nabina Das takes on the most human of our qualities, our yearning for story, and escorts us through poems that are also lyrical micro-narratives: from the very local—the flavors, colors and tastes of the market; the damp of an earthen floor; the fugitive beauty and ugliness of plastic litter—to the more abstract: earth, water, blood, losses, absences, breath, song, and silence. Anima is our first and best guide: a powerful, fearless entity who will take on any topic, including violent death, abiding love, pandemic loss. Das carries us, as she says in the double-meaning title of the second section of this work, to the narrative limits (and to the limits of narrative), consoling us in the final poem with her fugitive optimism: the image of hands catching light itself where fireflies make moving poetry of the night.

— **DEBRA CASTILLO**, author, translator, professor of Comparative Literature, and director of the Cornell Migration Studies minor.

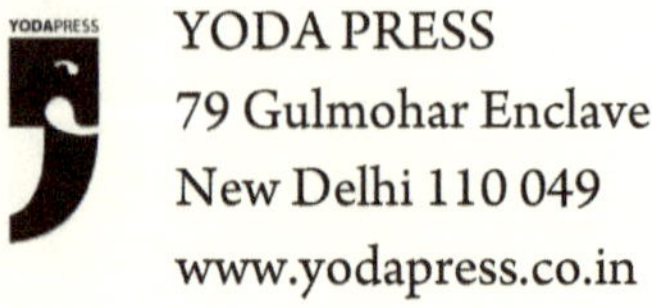

YODA PRESS
79 Gulmohar Enclave
New Delhi 110 049
www.yodapress.co.in

ISBN 9789382579670

Editor in charge: Chitraksh Ashray
Typeset by Saanvi Graphics, Noida
Printed at Atlantic Print Services
Published by Arpita Das for YODA PRESS

ACKNOWLEDGEMENTS

To the editors, journals, mentors, friends and family who steered me along by publishing some of the poems in their journals, and to those that kept my belief in poetry throughout a prolonged pandemic and personal travails.

For Raati, the luminous night of my days
And
My mother, who untaught me what little girls are taught.

CONTENTS

Contents

II: THE NARRATIVE LIMITS

III: A FEW THINGS OF CONSIDERATION

WHAT IS ANIMA SAYING TO US?

The poems in this volume were written more than half a decade ago. The need to connect with Anima began when I found myself getting increasingly bogged down by a system where the ones waiting at the periphery appeared to face unabated discrimination despite many promises by the government, prophets, saviours, and savants, and even those that say they patronize them. That last word—patronize—is discouraging, especially for women.

While bell hooks has educated us about her famous margin to centre theory, in our context, the margin often is kept from merging by several institutionalized aggressions. For example, someone told me recently that dissent is passé, and that the new world order is all about focussing on narratives that are more suitable for living room discussions or framed quotes on real and virtual walls; of flowers, clouds, kitties, food, and pretty faces. The personal should not get too political, the votaries urge.

Khana's tongue was severed for speaking up, and speaking truth and science. Flowers, clouds, kitties, food, and pretty faces. Even if she spoke and practised only those, she would not find her own space. Because she questioned.

My readers would have guessed it by now that these poems are starkly feminist and call upon men and women who see themselves not simply as radicals—to allude to the ignominy some people heap on the term—but also as those who will sing and celebrate speaking up. Anima, this way, is a clarion call to the feminine presence in all of our lives, nature's healing, and bonding between the stakeholders desiring peace and regeneration.

Anima is understood in the Western sense as psyche, an integral part of psychosomatic conditions as elaborated in Jungian psychology, the feminine principle present especially in men. If not outright empirical, it is at least an empowering notion in its application and discussion. But Anima did not arrive in that manner for me. It has been in my senses for a long time.

The very name 'Anima' was organically situated in my heart very early on, a name that belonged to my eldest aunt, a hero in many ways. It is illuminating indeed that the 'feminine' principle supposed to be present in a man, as one of the core archetypal ideals, was familiar to me as a woman of substance. Brilliant, astute, determined—the woman Anima was an embodiment of all that.

In the poems in this volume, Anima is also the quintessential woman spirit and body. She moves from towns to cities, hamlets to ports, jungles to highways, just as migration moves humans, seasons move herds of elephants or deer, and the earth's cycles move stars and the moon. Poetry and Anima are as inseparable as humans and their desires. We see here how the dismembered and dissected tongues, limbs, breasts, voice, laughter, and life fly back to join the women that Anima represents.

Nirmal Prabha Bordoloi's Assamese poems, with their ecstasy and strident language, are the mainstay of the writing here, her being a very early mentor of mine. My other influences—Tagore is an idea we cannot avoid, my father used to say as a critic of Tagore himself—are Kamala Das, Eunice De Souza, Kazi Nazrul Islam, T.S. Eliot, Maya Angelou, and Wislawa Szymborska. There are many others, no doubt. I have no hesitation in saying that my images and imagination get fired up while reading poignant work by Huzaifa Pandit from Kashmir, Mona Zote from Mizoram, Nandini Dhar of a critical space of thinking, Sophia Naz of a language of complex but lyrical metaphors, and Imtiaz Dharker of a diction traversing shores. Again, these are just a few examples from my own extensive poetic preferences. Translations have held me in their sway ever since I was a child learning to read and write. Of Nazim Hikmet, Mahmoud Darwish, Ko Un, Duo Duo, Akka Mahadevi, and Lal Ded, some have come early to me, some much later. I feel my writing becomes more fluid when I read more recent poets and my contemporaries, and forge identities with them.

The 'narrative limits' are, therefore, essentially a fluid limit that expands and encompasses what I perceive myself as—a poet, woman, flâneuse. The narrative limits have been within and without my poetic practice for more than a decade, so much so that I happen to carry the limitlessness of their narrative power as a 'cloak of invisibility', to use a Potteresque notion. Not simply invisibility but also indivisibility. The latter because as per the folk and fairy tales I grew up with, in(di)visibility was a charm one possessed, a key to the world of words and their power, and a tool to tread upon rough terrains of various discriminations.

Anima has been carrying her narrative limits both metaphorically and realistically if you care to know the Anima of this book—the poetic persona and the flesh-and-blood woman I know from my childhood. Storytelling, narrativization, and mostly, recounting reality through events recorded in current human memory—all this is what Anima carries on her tongue, her skin, and her sharp sensibilities.

Some of the poems individually published in magazines and journals have been read as laments. But they are mostly poems of loud questioning, as well as exaltation. About nature, about life, about feelings of rising from the depth to see the light above, about movements—how a feminine being moves across lands and seas, across the Milky Way and beyond the roads to perdition. Somewhat magical, but also a call to reality.

The 'limits' that we usually imagine to be hindrances are just signposts for Anima's leaps of imagination. Like a hurdle race participant, she sprints through life. She does not simply race to be ahead of adversities, but she also removes the hurdles from the way so no one else coming forth would stumble. This way, the narrative limits are how Anima soars by leaps and bounds and gives us poetry about the many ways she exists and women exist all around her— from margin to centre.

The second part of this collection—Narrative Limits—consists of poems that were written at different points in time, but all of them follow the tenor of the book. There is a sense of movement, a kinesis, an urge to be in the flow that one may read in these pieces where—from parts of Assam, where I was born and brought up and spent my childhood, to faraway cities and towns that sparkled to us girls like fireflies, and to distant shores that became home away from home—the footprints are seen all over, and keep leading further. It is a collective journey.

I've been aware of the problem of representation all along in writing this collection. The Anima of the imagined cities, towns, and villages is not represented by the Anima I knew as a child. The overlap or confluence of the individual I encountered and those that permeated my psyche is a strangely moving and sentient entity.

I cannot, of course, speak for a Dalit person, a minority citizen, a wronged, a violated, or a deprived woman, who all have experiences that are absolutely unique to them. But while writing these poems, I was sure I still needed to speak, mainly, of a woman's loves, losses, and longings. Hence, Anima can speak; she can lend her voice. This may seem to be a grand plan, but it is not so in my opinion. Far too many times women's stories just slip through the cracks. And if feminism is thought to be only a sob story, here's my take: the feminine voice of my Anima is crucial in celebration, in desire, and in surging forth.

We have Animas among us and also narrative limits that try to contain us all. It is an environment that needs regeneration and reimagining. The job of poetry is to bend the limits, breach them, and erupt in joy while creating our own narratives. Some of that euphoria has been recreated: flowers, clouds, kitties, food, and pretty faces. Not for living room reveries but for a collective narrative expedition.

Nabina Das
May 19, 2022
Hyderabad

I
ANIMA

Anima Stands in the Bazaar

This open bazaar is as old as my great grandmother. This bazaar was there when cows made dung from green grass. We still have shops that sell shiny toys, sticky sweets as well as vegetables and pickles, not everything gone to superstores. Come, I'll show you where to find the oldest seller. You can't tell whether it is a man or a woman. She-he has a face made of moon wrinkles and wears a long piece of white dhoti spun from Hatigorukhuwa. No, that place is really real. It literally means: eating-elephants-cows. I can't tell you who were the eaters of elephants or cows and if there weren't any, why that place would get such a quaint name. But I know names are not always a symbol of what you do or dispense with. Yes, you don't eat elephants or cows. But you let elephants cry as you chop down the forests. You make the cows die on your discarded plastic bags. Ah, plastic bags bring me back to the bazaar. We have beautiful ridge gourds here. Weighed and sold by she-he folks who could be my great grandmother's age. A story with each packet handed out. Buy it all, but don't cook the plastic.

All the world's a bazaar. I, Anima, will tell you next what the meat-seller is sharpening his cleaver for, when you visit here the next time.

Anima Takes a Stroll in the Park

It's cool in here with the Neem trees whose trunks are submerged in exquisite bush flowers. No, the gentle trees are not a motif for my conversation with you—that Neem branches are good natural toothbrushes, or eating Neem leaves will kill your stomach worms, or that Neem fruits can cause a fetus to fall. They're just here, the trees. Planted by a dead white man who apparently took some interest in this town. They say, he went to sit by the big tank on the south side every single evening. Not to watch the fish, or sunset, or hear the wind-driven ripples. A friend and clerk who wanted to write his biography decades later, and was refused by the big people of the town, said he used to sit by the tank to ponder its potential. Can the banks become a park or a walking stretch? Can the fish be harnessed partly elsewhere? Can the geometry of the natural tank yield any use for the water-starved little town lodged upstream of a great river? They say, the odd white man made the mistake of visiting the tank once in the afternoon. Women bathed there, also washed clothes. Someone threw a burning glass bottle on his window that evening when he had just put some waltz on the turntable. No, he didn't die. He was transferred. In any case, white men had mostly left our towns and cities. This man thought home wasn't a skin thing. But we learn with pain at times.

Oh, let me come back to the park. Neem leaves have covered the ground in piles. The town people plan to put a Hanuman statue by chopping some of these trees. I, Anima, will let you know if that'll keep the butterflies on the bush flowers still.

Anima Watches a Sure Death

I was certainly stiffer than him, my first dying man. Shocked to see a human go, a sure death as they say. I had wormed through a live wall of inert adults sniffling loudly in a closed dank room. Sniffling as though food had gone rancid and all. A hole in the fleshy forest of legs, hems and shoes let me in, and I stuck out scared like the bamboozled fly forgetting to do the routine buzz on the wall. Instead, I kept utterly quiet, not even a sigh. The tranquil form on the bed—no grimace—was heaped like buttered dough. Let's say, an octogenarian whose old-age bed was the only foothold from where he peeked at that unknown land, perhaps. Must mention I was a mere six-year-old watching a moment of parting. When a breath exits, long, for the very last time. His belly rose like that strange fish that pops itself up. Teasing us, it sagged, didn't again rise. The man, old, and sure in death, slept in his skin glowing bright as a new bamboo shoot in that afternoon light.

A sure death, did I say? Death is always in my head like tangles in the hair. Death is forever there for those that clamor for land and name. I, Anima, will tell you next time, why some people die very many unsure deaths.

Anima Speaks Two Tongues, Unforked

A certain erudite geographer-cum-anthologist is upset with me. I received a questionnaire and then a personal message. No, they don't write real letters anymore. Emails come sans frown or twitch of that sidewards muscle on the jaw. But I get the message anyway. The geographer-anthologist is a world-famous person, hence no arguing with him. Oh, they are all mostly *him*. I wouldn't imagine a severe woman masquerading as a kind global man just to tell me I happen to speak in more than one language. Where is your current geographic location, he asks me. I'm on a plateau, I say. They call it the Deccan Peninsula on the map. Sometimes I'm riding a slide down the Brahmaputra Valley, and sometimes, I hover in the sky. Ptolemy wouldn't have any issue with that, I feel. As for an anthology, can it hurt speaking in languages more than one or living in cultures that are like spices bundled together to steam with hearty summer greens or a winter squash or a spring sprig of drumstick? My good man has emailed me saying it makes categorization difficult for learned people. It forks up understanding.

I shut the noise off and listen to a river called Mora Bhorali in a calm town where Mian Bhai used to come rowing his boat, removing the hyacinth with his logi. Someone has to love the dead river, he used to say. I, Anima, of unforked tongues, will let you know soon the geography of sounds.

Anima Counts Footprints One by One

Here's a footprint! There, another. Oh look, another that has gone from the porch to somewhere unknown. Slowly rising from the side of the cowering bed, over a crumpled sheet, a pair has stepped hesitantly and then—dragged for a while till the kiss of the cold stairs drove it out of the house door. Still, these are footprints. Do you see the size of the shoes or the sandals? Are you saying a woman never wore shoes inside the house? Or is it bare feet? I'm kneeling down to see if the toes are showing on the damp of the floor like little sea conches that come and go, leaving their mark as though time was short. But for me too, this is deep and sad. Footsteps are growing like a sea. All we look for instead of a voice or warmth or even that presence around the space greeting us, enveloping us into her oneness. Then of course I look for more footprints, one by one, each of them. Some have left their skins on the gravel courtyard, some have slipped more than once on the turn of the tar road, while some have just become blood slush algae torn blossoms shallow smithereens of the late night dew.

I, Anima, plant my footprints around the homes, the bazaars, the summer-raged roads, the corners in the streets where hawkers spill oil and laughter but do not know who passed at night. I ask them if they know what the word 'disappeared' does to our bones, our hands and mud-soft stomachs. Will that girl Kumari return from the far forests to show us her untouched starched underskirt? Will that teacher Hajong come and say no worries, didibhai, my hands are not broken and I still can write? Have they seen the boy Burhan splitting grass with his teeth before he ran away to bite a bullet and is he back to his pranks or not? I, Anima, will track footprints till I can. Till I wake from the dream and tell you—look there they are, all of them wiping their soiled soles, resting at home.

Anima Holds a Name Tag in Her Hands

On my walks, I picked this solid metal strip from the hidden breast of the grass going grey. In the sky, the egrets were circling under the cloud like melancholy mendicants desirous of heavenly grace. My fingers became metal, became hard and cold, and the sky turned sallow as though thoughts from the horizon came rushing at me, at us, and the egrets. We soared or we thought we did. All we did was stare at a name. Somewhere gone to wars, or street violence, or seen cowering up like a child, and protecting its face. This was the borders, warned a few cattle herders. We graze the paddy, we make the dung, we walk the dividers on the fields. We also haul a dead cow off now and then when its neck gets pierced by a singing bullet. No name tag there. This is still the borders, warned the hen and egg vendors, their cycle-rickshaws hidden under tall water grass. Hidden like urgent semi-colons.

Jangam, Jangam, my little boy. Jangam, Jangam, my dead boy. The sal trees have seen a lot down the paddy lanes and muddy roadside drains. I wonder if that is a woman's voice trailing or just the old goose at the beel-water slowly covering up its bosom with the paani-meteka weed. I, Anima, am holding a book in my hands. Let me tell you soon how many name tags are on each of its war-torn pages.

Anima Asks of History a Few Questions

Do you know the taste of tamarind leaves? Do you know stale rice can make you swoon? Do you walk the town roads looking for old facades? Do you ever watch your face in a mirror? Do you ever wash? Do you sew little girls' clothes brought in torn and bloodied? Do you kiss fingerprints? Do you recycle cans and tins off nightly trucks carrying supplies? Do you peep in to see how dark is the black market? Do you try to catch a rainbow after the headline-making floods? Do you lend a hand to those who can never rise? Do you play with matchsticks only to light a fire or draw strict lines? Did someone ever call you skin-tanner, shoe-maker, shit-hauler, fish-scaler, carcass-burner and dead-soother? Were your foremothers from Dawki, Pathsala, Bhalukpung, Dhuburi or Hamren?

I, Anima, am of the elements. You, history, are of a tethered reality. Always salivating at the saucer of time. Always scrounging on bones that once sang deep songs. I, Anima, will return to you with another questionnaire. That, when we get even.

Anima Writes a Letter Home

Dear mother and father and old and young people of my home. Dear pets and weeds and flowers and footfalls. I write to you in a script speckled with time. I write to the language of a poet and many who chanted after her. I quote those verses which are laments, songs, praises and warnings. The laments are about not being of your skin, your tongue, your high heaven. The songs are about television screens, newsprint din, and the men with the megaphone going around shutting the windows down. The praises are to those that wear spotless clothes and hidden weapons, buck-skin shoes, and plastic faces. The warnings are about daring to speak, daring to say I am two languages not one, I am three faces not one, and I am a quarter bile not full. Dear people of my city, town, lane and invisible spaces, tell me how do I return to you? It is the night of the patient moon. But the doorkeepers are asking for proof that I lived here; the watchful voices are mocking my wandering toes, and the vigilantes are simply admiring their righteous claws.

I, Anima, stand bewildered in the midst of midnight's jowl. What is it, why is it that for many there's no home? It is Chaand Raat, the night of the moon. And a child's tearful whisper: Take me to Eid tomorrow, Ma, take me to Eid. I, Anima, ask you to wait for me to find the answer out when I carry the grasshopper home.

Anima Takes Back the Night

My cities are all bunched up like yesterday's flowers. Colors are visible but slowly fading at the lip of tea kettles. The petals shimmer their softness but are now steadily turning into newsprint and crumbs. The stems are coarse hands wrapped around sari ends and dupatta skeins. The hearts of my cities are pollen beds of invisible stings, tiny droplets of blood, and shards from unguarded paths. Where are you, night, when I need you the most? Where are the people cheering this solitary walk when my cities teach me names of each overpass pillar's piss spots and paan stains? This road was on the map the other day. That street was on the video just last month. My alley has been a gossip for many years, mouths dribbling of fears and lies. Did you know, they ask each other—a dragonfly-winged pori walks the night's backbone when she sings instead of sleeping. A high-heeled deity shows you her henna palms painted in the body's extract. A leather-jacketed back carries the moon and the stars that were thrown off in tied gunny sacks with women's names.

I, Anima, have been my own poet who walked the earth's ways for thousands of years. That poet died. The rivers lived. He wrote. The streetlamps swung in rhythm. I took a candle for the night cowering inside your filthy garages, sordid TV rooms, stinking gardens under your unkempt beds to show her—look night, the day is here.

Anima Walks Borderless

The forests are deep-cleft and dreaming. From Barak's beautiful sky-trees to upwards north of the dark-like ranges of a mountain kingdom I walk. Charaiveti, charaiveti, the distant locomotive wheels mumble running through the tunnels. And then I walk back to my Dihing where the journey had first started. The elephants are going to rest in their groves, no more hunted down by poachers. The speedboats are wrapping up their fishing nets in benevolence so the rivers are free. All hate is flying out on coordinates spanning our guide maps, and all love is fleeting in fast. How's this possible, you ask. We've seen vast graveyards of people dead. They were whisked away from homes, from children's sides, lovers' arms and disappeared for as long as one dew season went to the other. No one asked for maps for them. I remember the young girl whose country never came to her till she was of gray hair and mourning for her lost love. What is it, you ask. The sound of military boots at night in a new tongue. The red river redder with poison-bombed fish and weeping limbs. Charaiveti, charaiveti. The government map officers are here to scout a new route to send the hornbill flying to another border. I walk to send them back.

I, Anima, am a wandering body. From river to river, from one coalfield to another, dam to dam, I look for my own. I want my measuring tape, my own marker. I speak of woman body, turtle body, bird body. I speak a verse body across those cartographies. Our bard poet sang it in his silver voice across the red river: Mark

Twain with his body of stories, Gorky with his benevolence seeping down the murmuration of our spine. The bard's body in our quest, our long trudge back home. For I've let geography slip up through my river-sense. I'm stateless. I'm a jajabor.

Anima Calls Out to the Hemispheric Rhymes

Knowing you is like gauging the night sky. When the baked glow of the Deccan rises up to seek the rain, I remember how your voice rises. In slow movements, like tree limbs darkening in a mauve summer breeze. I look up and find a vastness vaster than my heart, a lit-up highway in the space. Is it gegenschein or airglow, I wonder. Possibly the bioluminescence of my firefly-limbs, the tiny movements that trickle right after a sowing song in this land. Who are those lovers that have lived inside you? I look, I search. The sky right after twilight has gathered its sari pleats. The colors are in a heady mix, signaling the low sun to take this rendezvous to the night's secret lair. I lapse into the dark-ink bowl of daylessness with the knowledge that your liquid air, your chunks of sunlight, and the flutter all over your body are just waking up to greenbluewhiting of our words. Exactly at those moments I also know you're gone deep into some wonderland crammed with animals and birds and ferns and figureheads. The salty mariner that you are, I know for sure you are sailing among the green foliage, maybe bogs, and most certainly, bushes and wilderness speckled with berries and insects. People write in vines, extracts, and long-drawn breaths. Are your words lonely logos across the dunes of time? They say the goddess of utterances makes imprints of them, grapheme by grapheme. Across the just-rained-in rocks and cheruvus, I read each word to actually see those fabulous lights in the night sky, smell the embracing undergrowth, and the compost, the leftovers of the raccoons, and the feathers of birds in their mercurial coming and going. I see you like an apparition flying under the sleeping

Mah Laqa Bai's shadow here. And I know you fleet in and out of your cove there, a fluid fish.

I, Anima, only see you better now with all the details of your world stitched back into mine now. It's surreal, the thought, but maybe your radio ether can pick up my breath at times, taproot timbre, staccato as my dreams, a noisy static like the germinal leaf's shudder. Now the hemispheres send rain—our words so darkly us, the charcoal yours, the mist mine.

Anima Sings and Still She Sings

Girl you will sing a song once all this is over girl you have been asked not to sing we know girl they held a matchstick under your tongue singed your voice box but girl you will speak up and you are speaking every time a hammer is coming down and cries are rending the air girl your clothes are torn to shreds but you have hundred limbs you can turn into leaves flowers dayflies sap from summer foliage girl you were asked to discard color so the blood surged ahead to color all where you inhabit and their weapons didn't know what to do girl you had been locked inside keys thrown off stones piled over your chest then girl you rose like the nimbus clouds girls your torn limbs rained again and again the dhaivat denied to all girls and girl you became belly tissues soft folds of the neck teenage breasts old skin of the buttocks the newborn vagina of the girl who has not seen spilled-ink trauma taunt or news headlines calling your name crowning you the fearless one but you were afraid girl and you didn't want candlelight vigil nor more bodies hanging in the solemn air girl you wanted to cross the streams in paradise to play tend work not become fodder of men in uniform girl you slept read demanded justice did not want to be jailed with pestilence eating your unborn offspring girl I call you girl because I'm tired of seeing only names waking people up which is not how sleep should end valleys rivers forests end or our poems end as though nights burning like bushfires so girl this is the moment to grab the minute's hand turn it into a fiddle a whiplash a sword a painter's stroke an innuendo a top spinning on the octave and bouncing down the curve for girl yes girl you girls you fairy dusts will rise like bodies beautiful bodies earthlike bodies and girl you will now sing and sing.

I, Anima, am only of the bodies of melodies and rage. When you get up girl and go to the realms of our sunshine our love and lusts that glitter like hidden gems when you sing to the plantains water chestnuts pond-koi when you raise the pancham to where our spines tingle, I will turn into the force the bulwark our girl hands girl feet our girl bodies mapping all the maps.

Anima and the Ballad of Breath

And this is how one is truthfully mournful when at moondown the gaunt sky strides across a field of edible rot, fishes out bodies big and small, as though marinated slugs from a manhole. This is how it's then if moans rise accidentally over leathery forms that call themselves children of dead corn, poisoned mushrooms, this is how it is to hear a sigh that devours meanings. Air going to nil, heart beats going to stony silence, pyres burning not just bodies but our dreams. And so this is how we make sure all's fine—when you ask where the ventilator switch is kept in cold death wards, to lead us through a corridor stacked with the suffering crowd, towards a grave that never tasted bran of our hands. Did you see a twister felling lonely trees limbs fruits rocks and milling cadavers that blinked once to pray for air, then died? This is how you make sure it's easily done. This is how it is then—your wily game forcing us to wager our orchards and farms, airdrop bundles you throw on the departed, click and bait from your dog-friendly sofa to dole out rations in the name of nation.

I, Anima, know this is how you tell your infected mind that we still resist and stun. Yes, we do, we holler at the causes changing touches and shapes, and humans and grains. We rise from our gone-bodies, we reinvent the joyless earth, atom by atom. We make every breath a promise that we will bring you down. Our ballad of breath a sweeping storm over your calumny, an earthworm turning the soil into a new mix, our lungs germinating leaves for children, our victory runs.

Anima of the River's Arm

Evening falls. The big bend of the river has everyone in its thrall like the first virginal blood. The sun has also shed its vermillion sap in the deep deepness of the water's pull. The blueing of the faraway hillocks has my thighs shiver where your mouth left the half-moon marks. I walk, walk the path of fireflies till the great river bend subsides with our passion. From Luitporia songlines to the edge of our soft consonants. From our sounds uttered in repose, half-sounds of di-di-di or ti-ti-ti that reverberate like first words. All river-words when love rains like di or ti. And we're like the night, yet to be born into the day. We've seen our syllables roll like dew drops on the lotus leaf. Evening falls. Shadows fall on my face like the whirl of the river dolphins grayed in love and grace in their little eddies. And then the dawn call of fishermen stirs my hair, the char silt sifting its grains through each strand. I rise from their ecstatic jikir: Ali, Ali, ya Ali. I exist here, in this air of no fixed prayer, in this vast swelling of no divinity, in this lover's arm of a river where no invocation is needed. I walk past the canvases of jakois set in the shallow water where the fish dream.

I, Anima, am of no mantras, no deities, no one source. Come walk with me and be my roots, come swim with me and be the in-between mist of the Umananda mornings. Come be the goddess who jumped into the river and raised a fist before she swam away. Come to flow.

Anima Writes a Goddess Story

The deity is earth. The goddess is flesh made of earth. Every autumn, she's brought back to journey through the interminable. Every season sees her face as though a fallen flower on the golden soil of oblivion, every tear a dewdrop on it.

Durga is going to her mother's place on a rickshaw. At the turn in a dark alley, suddenly three men come upon her. They push the ragged rickshaw puller down from his seat. Scuffle and scream. Then quiet. Stop.

Durga is late for office. One of those days she feels sick and falls behind on her schedule. Male colleagues keep cracking the 'monthly' joke on her in the lunch room while she swallows a pill and prepares for a late evening over files. Stop.

Durga is not allowed to cross the threshold of the big house in her village. She can chop the crops, shear the corn, gather the bundles, clean the wheat grinder, but can never enter the big-house kitchen. She can wash their clothes, clean their buckets, but never touch the big-house drinking water pots. Alien to touch, she can become a body for the big-house men. But a nobody to be counted as human in birth or death. Stop.

Durga is a widow with no Shiva for protection. No sons or army of earthly fans. She says she'll grant everyone's wishes by sweeping corridors, scrounging dishes, dusting homes, cooking food, even bearing the houseowner's long glances behind her while she mops the floor. Stop.

Durga is in love. Mahisha is the man. But she's whisked away and locked in a room without food or water. She is threatened with dire consequences. Even death. Mahisha must die. She should poison his tea or else the clan men will hack his head. 'Love jihad?' Durga feels she's going mad in this din and light and nag. Make me a goddess, I'll do it, she yells at last. Stop.

I, Anima, am no Durga. But I am the woman you have seen many times, the fallen autumnal flower on the golden threshold of your lies and lusts. Come rise with me, don't raise me, just stand and see me rise. The deity will watch even if his eyes are blinded. The goddess will become a woman again, free of all woes, unclasped of men. No one to say stop.

Anima Wakes up Tejimola

Now is the hour for Tejimola. She is back from the dead. From the many deaths. From the blood in the pumpkin vine, from the splintered limbs in the rice pestle, from the torn ligaments tangled in the branches of the trees. Now is the hour Tejimola walks the winding path back home. The hills are winding, the sky is a ferry across the tumult of the mind. Life stops. Life waits. Life is back. The pumpkin vine grows in the belly of the evil mother. Once eaten, the seeds splinter and splutter, become thousand eyes. They see through the belly skin. They peek through the navel. The eyes. They hurry out in the bloodstream and scream. The rice powder from the heavy pestle falls like dew at night. The river mist settles into the slums and shanties lining the road she takes. Tejimola has walked through the checkpoints. Tejimola has stood along the truck routes her face painted, her limbs akimbo on a bonnet. Tejimola is dreaming of the faraway sea, right of the country liquor shop, left of the hutments where women screamed in terror. Sea, a sea, many seas. The ship is not coming to take her back. The vine is not going to flower again. The mortar will not fall asleep.

I, Anima, can feel Tejimola waking up inside me. Across acid fields, shanties, human dumps, torn dreams, electric wastes, I walk on. If you hear someone saying life in a sunrise voice, you must know it is us. Two women gone to three and four and more. We're waking up to take on the tangle and the tide.

Anima Sings to Earth and Death

The day breaks like a forgotten prayer. Everyone scurrying to work as usual—kids to school, harried people in ill-fitted clothes to office, and vendors and shopkeepers to their stations and stalls. Footfalls are markers in the arid wind. Inside the heart of this strange apocalyptic flower called life, human bees are rushing to the poison nectar. Big cars are outsmarting smaller vehicles, smoke and dust gradually taking over the morning freshness. Perhaps this freshness will be bottled and sold in some near dystopic future. Honks and screeches taking over the faint morning murmur of leaves, of what remains of leaves and trees. Textbook makers are struggling to print leaf pictures. No one knows what a gold-filigreed Amaltas looks like. Or a starry-white mogra bloom. Is it shaped like a bird or a spider, they ask. Being a flâneur doesn't help because the roads are not walkable, of what remains of paths called roads. We've walked and stood and looked ahead to see only the abyss beyond the smog. We haven't seen the hands waving in a frantic plea. Everyone wants to live in a smart city but no one drags out of the hole the humans sinking deep in our stinking urban bogs. Everyone thinks a selfie with toxic waste and floating diyas will save our souls. The river has swollen in its joints with sludge and clouds of fumes. The daybreak has gone to a dense night, one that speaks only of ruins.

I, Anima, will turn into a bog light. I'll fall in thousand showers on your paths. On your broken shards, plastic wastes, human excreta, metal scraps and collective junk. If you look for the North Star, you'll find me stuck to your sleeve, a woman-heart ripped out. Aglow. Leading kindly.

Anima of the Old Dancer City

The city is an old danseuse, the traffic her broken anklets. Her faded skirt sweeping across the green paddies where tears have mingled since decades. The city is the lost dubori grass. It has bent down looking for its own shadow till the root of oblivion. The Nilachal held her headdress, the hornbills brought her girdle feathers, and the river a gentle swipe of her limbs. She has danced since eternity, her legs astride the flyovers, her heart pasted on to mine. I, Anima, want to reach out and ask the city-kunwori, how much longer, dear girl? How much longer before you dance away to fatigue, to cover up the crinkles, the stretch marks, the scars and strife of generations, the migrant shame? How long before we see our foremothers arise from their ashes? The city is Laxmi Orang, her breasts darkened by the afternoon sun. The city is a fugitive. It's running away, fast, fast, in a frenzy. From Beltola to Christian Basti to Athgaon to far away beyond the river's bend, the city is a nameless traveler. Her ankles bared and clothes smudged with soil, saliva, slivers of bloodied flesh. The city is the bihuwoti shamed for mixing her language and her song, her mekhela turning into newsprint. The newsprint turning into lumps in our tear drops. There's an order not to shed tears in this city. But the city is matsyakanya. She has known only water. Water of tears, sweat and melting of dreams. Her liquid hopes slowly rising to touch the skies.

I, Anima, am also a city. I'm a city with Bagurumba steps. I'm an old danseuse city courting time. There'll be a season I'll build myself with water hyacinth step-moss eastern-star fish-eggs and all that grow into pillars and props. I'll stitch myself brick by brick to melt them all down again like a lava flow. I'll free my mermaid's tail from the concrete and slide back into the river of blue dreams. I will free this city.

Anima Speaks the Silent Tongue of Women

There's a song in my heart tissues. A song about the moonlit fort. As a little girl, like all little girls, I've heard that all little girls are captive there under the moonlight. The moonlight promises to preserve them. Melt their fat and scabs. Cleanse them of any dark shadow. There is silence. Nimaat nixa—the speechless night. I've heard about the voiceless daughters of the wordless nights. Our nimaati koinas. All of them brides, daughters, princesses, witches, healers down the ages. The moonlight promises them silence. All little girls have courted silence ever since the moonlight has assured them of a white shadow and shelter. All little girls are still playing a tune, the only way they make sure not to forget the alphabet of their hearts. There was a song. A song about their song and now this is a song about the songs the little girls sang. They're still silent and they cannot be seen. The melody rises from unseen choruses. The notes touch the girls. Girls who have eyes that speak. Their tongues don't. They have limbs that wish to step outside the fort but they cannot. The melody rises beyond the dead of the night, touches the huts of the city, dips its toes into the beels choking with multiplex rubbles, plastic waste, and squeezes past the urgent paths losing themselves in the maze of the mall-ridden thoroughfares. Aailata is walking sleepy-eyed to work, tasting only rancid rice. Chitro is picking up her dung bucket, a baby in the other arm. Jahanara is counting money thrown to her flesh after a night of silence. I don't know any of them, yet, I'm all of them.

I, Anima, will not wait for any prince to come. I'm tearing up storybooks to free the mute woman-in-waiting. She catches my shirt blowing up in the sky reddening the tropical sun. She follows the gulls. She will flow after the river. She will tell me, you, Anima, will lead me to the sound. Then we'll write a story together.

Anima Dreams a Home

Take a fistful of sand. Sprinkle it in the wind. Start tracing the grains on the floor using lines. Those songlines, lines from the furrows of your mouth, lines from the fold of the eyes. We've come down the hills, across the map lines, slept flat-bellied on the plains to dream. To let the saliva form the rivers in the dust. And we raised ourselves on the land like we raise a home. They have dragged our daughters out to the forest, our men to the bloody pits, our dreams to the ravines. All of us lay inside a hut and dreamt of a sun, a home, and a river so lucid that it washed us clean every night. We dreamt every night and rode the waves. We went in grass hiding in the season's grace from all that broke our homes, our hen sheds, our beautiful arum stalks from the pond side. We lay and lay to see us start singing in the living room, the notes lighting up the hanging lamps and spinning curtains. But is this a home? Is this what they call the khwabgaah, the dream vessel where our minds sail? I've seen the mortar cling to people's sinews, cloying their hearts. I've heard the cries from within cells of bricks and barriers. So now we take a fistful of sand, a sprinkle of cement from our body, a layering of bricks pieced from the kiln of our burning desire. The ground shifts and rivers burst forth on the roads that stopped us from finding home.

I, Anima, will sing the song of razing the prisons to the ground. We'll raze the high walls and the cold concrete dungeons, all detention camps. They will never hold dew drops. Once broken, they'll become dough on the moist soil. Our home will rise from the bread we will knead together. The bread of freedom, the bread of fearlessness, the bread we'll share with all across the table.

Anima Speaks to Harud

The sky has turned ochre in my town. From soorkh to zard. From fiery red of the once-spring to the pale melancholia of losses. Even bogs are turning turbid because somewhere the voices are imprisoned. The voices cannot escape above slimming themselves up in the razor-thin air. Harud, please, show your face, Harud. Quiet households are watching the footprints of the fog, that autumnal breath of the ones who only wait like shadows. Quiet like our dreams. The only noise is of the hopes rising—rising like crystal flakes of fairy glass, but alas! They come crashing down on the hard ground. Another Kristallnacht. Harud, you're a season. Harud, you're the heart's loving stain. Harud is when the pancham note goes to saptam and breaks into a night of mournful vigilance. We sing it in vain. But fear not, dear Harud. Your colour is our spleen, our bile, our murdered kin's tranced face. We call it holud, the colour of pain and agony. Behind concertina wires and military barricades, Harud, you've tiptoed into our hearts. We call this gushing flight halodhi, the essence of our rage and love. Halodhi is little girls coming to dip in for the senses to be dowsed in gold. Holud is sudden birds giving wings to men who know even the sun won't melt them down. Listen! There's a sound of phone suddenly come to a life of language. There's a sound of a bird pecking at the apple gone to grass. There's a sound of janaza where the dead slowly rises to watch over the living. There's a sound of firing but the wound remains invisible to gods. Harud, my Harud, hold our hands. Holud will lift you up in the yellow-green air. Halodhi will wash you with goldshower love.

I, Anima, of the eastern star, will wear ornaments of the fallen leaves today. It's time we turn everything back into soorkh. One by one we'll sprout flowers from our limbs. Autumn, grass, fallen fruits and sap. Each a flower to become thousand eyes. Autumn, heart, dreams, songs. Each a flower clamouring to eat the lies.

Anima Traces a Pestilence

The air breathes heavy. The girl watches the pestilence rise with the vapour to mingle in the air. The girl stares inside the washroom mirror marking the minutes of the passage of breath. Each breath licking the glass, then trying to slip out of the window, sneaking out of the heavy door. The girl continues to breathe, the mirror marking a rhythm her heart is trying to remember. Something is dropping in on her, either the disinfectant spray from the inner ducts of the air-conditioning or the outspilled soap bubbles still carrying the synthetic fragrance in the washroom air. Is it peace, is it reverie, or is it the simple feeling that language is mostly vowels when you lose your tongue, or teeth, or lie hungry and battered on the roads? Pestilence is our inhumanity. Our own bone-crushing apathy where limbs are tendrils gone to infection. The mirror reflects it. A selfie of the world around. The girl watches, the world breathes heavy.

I, Anima, am today a reflection of all the thorns inside the rose-blush lungs. I'm the blue mask of our times, the choke spreading in our throbs. I'm also the flow that folds in all hearts, a spring water the girl facing the mirror is searching. There's a Swan Lake unfolding, the wings taking swipes, water and particles falling in bits and pieces like grace. I, Anima, will cleanse her tarnished hands, the crinkled brows, the breaths gone awry from our own squander.

Anima Rearranges a Nostalgia

Shoes, old clothes, dismembered plastic cutlery, torn leaves, upturned buckets, caved-in hutments, hole-punched asbestos roofs, shredded blue tarp sheets against the rains, and a sniff of autumn that feels like a perfume from another time. Even the sun is caught in the crepuscular sickle that shears all our pretence. The slow grace of caterpillars, the mayfly roosting on pores of algae growing like our myths, that one leaf dangling by its petiole from a bark too dark for us to see—all just a punctuation in the human clock. Ek bagal mein chand hoga ek bagal mein rotiyaan. Why is there a blood-soaked train track and half-moons of our follies garlanding the times? What are these dreams of food bags showering down in stale petals over gaping mouths? Where will the road take them, how far, when there's not a shirt on their back? Where is home, where is hearth, where is warmth? Shoes, tattered clothes, plastic life in smithereens, rotten leaves, broken buckets, roofless holes, the flightless imagination of a time wrapped around like the blue tarp. Women and babies, and men and mothers in a huddle, slowly becoming artefacts of our failures.

I, Anima, keep rearranging the pieces of this nostalgia. No one will remember because nostalgia is a flower that dies at dawn. Because nostalgia walks miles along the highways. Nostalgia falls in broken pieces over our homes, news screens, print fonts, crumbling facades of what we call shame. There will be a day when each petal of this nostalgia will bloom redbluegreen. Each half-moon will come alive in hungry stomachs. Ek bagal mein chand hoga ek bagal mein rotiyaan.

Anima Paints in Three Colours

Here's a palette. Here are colours. Here are brushes and a little chisel to mark your boundaries. You can see the colours and call out their names. There is white. There is green. And there is the colour of soil. White is water split rocks semen tendrils and the gullet in its crevices. Green is blood memory dawn sky and shuffling feet from line to line to fence to fence. The third color is a deep cry yellow amber soul and anthills. The painting starts sputtering like jeeps electric nodes dying hearts on the body's cradle, and that is when the colors bind and unbind to start our history lessons. Lessons in flesh and death and violent dreams. Three is no longer one, one is no longer a trinity, and the canvas is etched with frantic rhymes.

I, Anima, am the body on which we will write the next chapter. A textbook of resilience, a manual of stronger cogs, a manifesto of deeper revolutions to bring the colors home. Call it race, call it face, call it your passport—this painting is not for auction or a price.

II

THE NARRATIVE LIMITS

New Words in This Grammar

If I ask you to search the tin box of your memory[*]
I know you'd be first looking for the locks of your memory.

Hear something rattle inside like coins? Imagine their spark?
Hark, listen carefully, there are talks of your memory.

The very word memory is such an anathema to me—
Top it with more inanity: Yes! Shocks of your memory.

Comfort was holding hands, kissing. We dallied sans care.
Inside my brittle heart now, alas, only knocks of your memory.

Social distancing, lockdowns—new words in this grammar!
Here's what Navi lives by, arranging the blocks of your memory.

---

[*] *'In the tin box of your memory, a coin of comfort rattles' is a line in Imtiaz Dharker's poem 'Purdah'.*

Nabina Das

Eunice Dreams of 'Miss Louis'*

She dreamt of lush forms, waves
Of gigantic desires, and then made
A resolution. Love was beyond
That blurry line, minus this sickness.
Lovers were just assembled there
Where the water flowed clean.
She dreamt of honey toast with
Less of anxiety. Also lovers. Those
With faces scrubbed like museum
Paintings. Skin soft like scrambled eggs.
Those that were sanitized in their heads.
At midnight she saw the desires creep out
Of bedrooms and kitchens from all
Around her. The night birds screamed
As though in orgasm. Her red lips
Shaped the descending solitude:
Better than government number curves.
Brighter than all economic projections.
Then she dreamt of chiseling puns
Of slight flights. Where she let verbs
Become staircases, to slide down,
To clamber on to, heavy-breathed—
So everyone knows how she makes love
Sound like the words were fire: they fight and win.

––––––––––––––––––––––––
* *A poem by Eunice De Souza.*

The Song of Kamala Sundari

They came in a boat for Kamala Sundari
sieving water layer by layer
when the wind rose
the oars were legs, also their hands when stretched

The boats they built later were not for her
the waters they slashed was a mingled song
Kamala Sundari stared in death when they came
her face marigold, her body wooden planks

Badar Badar Ghazi Ghazi
Badar Badar Ghazi Ghazi

And Kamala Sundari gazed outside for long
a little window past the Haflong orchards
past the Cherrapunji clouds of clamor
past those roads where boats became legs
water was dust and greens were tangled lines
amid all, her steps each a slash on the seas

Legs that grew to be tall buildings,
little buildings, concrete buildings,
legs that became pillars, posts and pipes
standing in an acid moon they were shadows
with legs that forgot to have their feet
toes that could wriggle out of mossy pools

Badar Badar Ghazi Ghazi
Badar Badar Ghazi Ghazi

And Kamala Sundari sang first in a whisper
she then sang out loud, forgetting the words
because words were off on their legs by then
becoming oars, rowing boats in a frantic grace
they were all expected to be so beautiful
just like Kamala Sundari, were expected to go
from town to town, boring into root to root—
Oh so frantic, oh so hundred-oared.

Tejimola, Live

They say:

She had walked the path of hundred algae
the path of two hundred nights of limb-breaking rice-pounding
pestle
the path of five hundred miles of shackles that later turned to
flowers

Later is a word that was cowering in the shade
under the cowshed
needling through the haystack blades
later mumbled later, O father, O mother who isn't
the flowers later turned into questions in bunches
that all girls ask

Tejimola says:

Tej in my name is blood, the color of a gash
tej runs fast like old red swirls of the man-
river who sleeps while torn flesh and ashes churn in its pull
tej is where mangled little girls are bound with silent names and
no love

O father, O mother who isn't, look at me
the pumpkin of your discarded vine is my head
the orange, the red, the seeds of desire and folly
look at me and see where the bloom is, the plum
and the soft warmth of my cheeks

find me floating in your prohibited dreams
your seamless hatred and the lotus that lusts
what's love what's union what's the binding of flesh, dear father
dear stepmother,
what's the longing that lingers on a hope that this blood-girl will
live, long, long, long, very long?

The Political Lives of Terrorist Wives and Other Insignificant Women

It is that deep-belly start of an autumn sunrise by the ghost
moon's side
And the Neem and Bokul are overlooking the forms still to bake
under the sun
The kawoi fish bodies asleep with the elixir of rice and millet of
their pain
All of it from the nights that visited their loves and then a sudden
loss of air
I now see by the egg-cracked dawn sky how low the clouds shift to
faces
Soon the faces will wash and scrub and take their daily wares,
parceled fares
Sweet chai swirling in the throat and ill-fitted blouses on bodies of
prose
Mint and mangosteen nudging into sour berries tout with sweaty
coins
And they'll rush into your sacred spaces, trampling on petals,
holiness and all
They've asked me not to billow my gaze and rest the pen on my
hunches
We imitate each other: we sit on hunches by every moon's side of
wane
Only, they by the paddy or the kohuwa's ears, while I on my
purveyor's seat

Looking far into the bricolage of urban mass and fungi of military
posters

I hear the women mumble about men and calves and pigs that wander slow
Deep; and rising over the penitent dust they flounder till they find their sleep

It's the same story over and over again seeping through the custard apple
Through miles and miles of gunrunning, strangers' footwear on flood-licked steps
Have they found their loves, I wonder. Or has the verse given them rights?
We imagine rising above our lives in nervous flights along Nagaon-Moriani roads

Faiz, I've seen more!

Should there be more crucial
things other than love to fight
for, more sorrows, more crises,
while we fold the laundry with
our tidy lives, to abide by rules?
Should I be complaining less
about curdled milk, cold soup,
and the clock galloping fast?
About why I spell love at times
as 'wave' or even 'give', even if
I feel I haven't given enough
yet, or haven't kissed the crest
of your waves? Should there be
only loss to account for? We weep
because we'll carry hurt, then
say to the world—'No! Do not
ask for the same sort of love
that we spoke of once many
years ago; drank from its core.'
But, Faiz, I've now seen more.
So perhaps it is time right now
to leave aside all fire and gore,
loosen up the revolutionary
fatigues and boots and seek
that soft niche where love lives.
Beyond barricades and slogans
it is time to find the hour when
the world can really change.

And I can exclaim—'Oh why!
Not one bone in this, my body,
is as long as your lone femur!'
Let's now count sorrows other
than just love. Gifts never given.
Receding waves that life leaves.

aubade: of days and breaks

i've never loved anyone from silchar
i've kissed no man from the valley
i held no woman's hand from the bazaar

they say small towns don't generate love
but that's not true

i've loved small towns better
than their tin roofs those with the smells of broken shells
from receded seas
even the ones that are sprinkled with the sweat of moss at dew time

true, i've never kissed a man who lived inside silchar's green
plantain skin
i never hugged a womanly body everyone pulped in their dreams
but they say not loving brings good luck too
if you just pretend to love small towns like silchar and its humid
firebirds
its small life stories, morning paanta-bhaat, nightly fishing boats,
bangle-adorned shops
opening up in fajr prayers

yes, just pretend you are the fish
while the lovers are your constant lit-unlit fireflies extinguishing
in the mornings

i've done just that for love.

Nabina Das

The Many Uses of the Word 'Great'

This perch is green
The way they want it green
In poetry and sylvan movies

This plate is full
The way we dream it full
Across tables of insouciance and gilt

My mother tells me of the great
Flood of North Bengal and streams
Of women and men begging to be
Saved following into the towns
Bloated cows and stomachs

My father held a chilled whiskey glass
Talking about skeletal forms from
The great Bengal famine. They came
Asking for rice water in the tone of a torn
Banjo. He didn't drink, he cried

What is a pandemic, the little one
Asks and everyone ruffles
Through great big books

The news screen beams
The great betrayal. Like hope,
Our indifference flickers

I've used the word great here
A number of times. What remains
Is how people die, before words do

Healing amid Ruins

If this is the end, then let there be a light in ruins!
Let it glimmer like a star, this little light in ruins*.

Ruins have always been my habitat, my refuge.
Did you ever notice how I shine bright in ruins?

One day this world must clean up and breathe. Must
live. Or perish in hatred. Lose its might in ruins.

The taboo word is 'contact', please beware!
Mind the healing touch. Set farther your sight in ruins.

Every home is a jail if the people aren't free—
Whether sickness or revolution, we alight in ruins.

I want to love, want the shackles to crumble down.
How do I call off the bluff, the sorry blight in ruins?

Ah, sedition is the password in His Master's Voice!
Let's heal cell by cell, Navi, let's step right within ruins.

---

* Refers to 'A Light in Ruins Glimmers Like a Star…', the first line of
  the Ukrainian poet Yunna Morits's poem 'A Light in Ruins'.

Come Eat My Lotus-Heart

Beloved, I want you to be my lotus-heart.
Step across, come see my lotus-heart.

Germination has deserted this firmament.
So only you can come free my lotus-heart.

The bazaar no longer has our footprints—
Don't now make me flee my lotus-heart.

TV sets blare inside homes. Can they hear
What birds speak in glee: 'My lotus-heart!'

How to again kiss? We cannot even touch!
Did I lose, Navi, in this melee, my lotus-heart?

Flowers of Light

If one shouldn't place flowers of light in their hands, then what's
to be done?*

Give them the Constitution our Babasaheb wrote, that's to be done.

Even the quarantined trees in this city have started shedding tears.
Even the shackled working hands do what gets to be done.

Food packets, milk for infants, a shelter for the calloused backs—
Why call a djinn to act? We all know this has to be done.

The elites are writing newspaper op-eds, calling it a new conflict.
A lot was unscrupulous, so much was undone. Still lots to be done.

Fake news, police batons—the damn country is a sinking boat!
People who've never kissed or loved tell us what's to be done?!

My love is for azaadi. Not razor wires. The beloved awaits
freedom.
Place the flowers of light in migrant hands, Navi. Indeed, that's to
be done.

---

* *Refers to 'Amidst a New Conflict' by Narayan Surve. The last stanza in
this poem goes: 'If one should not place flowers of light in their hands:
then, what's to be done?'*

In Happiness, Tremble

The day, each day, is itself.
The way it dawns and
then heart-steps itself
to the brink of folding in.
We think it is in happiness
that it trembles on leftover
soup bowls, rice plates, din
that we make. All the while
we suppose we're living.
We want a clean sky, air
smelling of detergents on
our hands. The spinach wilts
with too much attention.
Happiness tiptoes over
the terrace to find us tremble.
The blanched horizon sinks
before the birds are aflutter.
Whose happiness is it really,
we forget. Prepare a list
again to stay alive, stock food,
exchange bodily concerns.
There's a tremble rising slow:
The day, the night, the vast
space with stars, our stares
meditating shoelaces, old
underwear, and all knick-knacks
we'll soon replace afresh. Write
another blatant ode to happiness.

Limits

It began with examining specks
lying over the floor. As though gems.
Our nail waste, tangled hair, dead skin.
Dead bits of ourselves showcased.
Like spent dragonfly wings. Life
in its limitlessness kissed by death.
But a kiss is like kintsugi. It repairs.
Also, it doesn't believe in limits. Mostly
remaining off limits in its morphology.
But it began with gauging each square
foot of the space we tend to step on.
How much of this air? How much vacuum?
What inches accord us our coordinates,
were the questions. As against each
footprint we left on the wet surfaces
of our dreams, life became microscopic.
Measure the limits of life in coffee cups,
the poet said! You did too. When alone
we tried saying loving words from
another era in history. You showed me
how to hold a butcher's knife right. Left
me with my own throbbing heart.
It began with dicing time, love, life, as
they died. As sparks in flight. All night.

Existential

The lone garlic pod is a monk
sitting over the kitchen counter.
A silent oblong ascetic. It chants
all possible incantations
against harsher times. Green
shoots are just reminders
of its absolute indivisible
powers. Slow preservation
but steady escalation on
the path of what we humans
call life. It is draped in white
because, no, not a shroud,
it is just the ample tenacity
of the alabaster form. Stoic
and firm on the cool granite.
What seems slow to the eye
is actually a grand resolution
that past all ages of the earth,
this pod will cradle in its inside
our capers, apathy, and pride.
We'll write ditties to the moon,
call our sighs poems. The pod
will shake its head. It'll preserve
its sharp cynicism for harsher times ahead.

When my letter quoted: 'Main tenu pher milaangi...'*

I folded up the letter
With that line at the end:
I will meet you yet again.

The truth is, the full moon
Has stirred into the ink
Your name. Just as water.

Does water not stay
In one place, while love
Flows victorious? Your name.

The other truth is, zuwa,
They've barricaded Kashmir
Again. I've never even met you.

While everyone's smiling
At the Covid moon, I don't
See where the light shines.

Because they've killed
Another and darkened
The ink of news headlines.

---

* *The title is a reference to a famous poem by Amrita Pritam.*

The truth is, zuwa, we
Will never meet. Not
Till the letters find home.

Ask where is the home.
Ask where are the post offices.
Is the blood red, or are mailboxes?

When the body perishes, does all
Else perish? The dead comes out
In the germinal street, a shoot.

Keep the flower on the nozzle
The gun salute tuned to the heart.
Then we will meet yet again, zuwa.
This letter now in your name.

Nabina Das

Speak to Us of Clothes

Know them by their clothes, said
the dark lord. And the trees shed
their leaves. The horizon went dark
in shame. Skin got hemmed in quick.

When Billy Collins had said:
'The complexity of women's
undergarments in nineteenth
-century America is not
to be waved off,' what must
have intrigued the white
male poet is how easily women
avoid the word garb when
they talk about what to wear.

You don't have to be good
and wear only the white of lilies,
cotton of our mother's dreams
or the right color of our leaders.

Our leaders are the Clorox
and the Lysol trying to get
up close and personal while
we can only wear longings.
Lust to die full of questions.

The weaver said, 'Speak
to us of Clothes.' We spoke
of being seen. So they know
us by our clothes. Underpants,
bra, girdle, pants with the long
and the short of it all, also skull
caps. Finally, our skulls smashed.
Finally, our skin, the only cloth
we could douse in the fuel
of a rebel heart. We could light
a c-o-n-f-l-a-g-r-a-t-i-o-n. That word
has a long spelling. And a long spell.

Perfection as Immunity

The woman was perfected[*]
In some dreams alone. Or in prose
Written by men throbbing in the breeze,
Imagining her chiffon. Her rags
Were invisible. The way she folded
Within the petals heaped over her
When she was dead. The face
Got perfected by the painter's brush.
A whitewash was the only magic
Touch. No one saw the pain lines
Or the struggle for immunity. Her viral
Desires. At the end of the day she lay
Embossed in cleaned cutleries,
Fine cotton serviettes. Perfected
For the next book or silver screen.

---

[*] 'The woman is perfected' is the first line of Sylvia Plath's poem
titled 'Edge'.

'For Calling the Spirit Back from Wandering the Earth in Its Human Feet'*

Nights have a special place
in our awakening. It's from
the night that we came. Wandering.

Who's the Believer then? Shall we pray
in the dark watches of the night
when daylight shows only misery:
the practice of tahajjud, in the darkest night.

The day is all lime-sprinkled. Laundry
Soaking like our hearts in fear. Disinfectants
Wrapping us as we seek barakat.

Shab-e-Baraat, Shab-e-Baraat—
the Night of Forgiveness flowers
faster than flames.

Send us dua, night birds sing.
Send us the extracts from
your Lailat-ul Dua, the sap of your deeds,
say day flies stuck on human spoils.

Amid EMI flats and concrete rises
Burnt smell of broken hearths

---

* *The title is a line from a poem by Joy Harjo.*

Footfalls driven out of homes.
See how our past catches up with us.

Make this the night of records,
for every night. The day of gathering
bounties each day. Call the spirits back.

Today, my eyes like Christ's eyes
cannot find enough moist earth
to rest the wounds of my people.

Broken Mermaids

Because everyone's saying what
I want to say. Already they
Have the metaphors sieved
The similes sun-dried and spic
And span. The alliterations have
Brushed their alligator teeth. Puns
Have pre-heated their cozy
Impact. Like warm buns they sit
Awaiting the honey of the tongues.

Only the woman doesn't speak but all else talk about her
The little hurts, the abrasions die like moths on the lamp.

Just too much sense for me to hear
And store in my head. Still, I dip
A finger or two in this mad swirl
And taste the jelly. Tastes alright
Like blank sighs, a bit tart like love
Also bittersweet when milk burns.
That reminds me of how milk
Is linked to humankind, as though
Humankind was a big, kind cow
Mooing out gently its synecdoche
And hyperboles. Now of course
I'm reminded of cows, the animal
To go down in history as part myth
And part reality after Griffin, the Roc
Or the Centaur. The cow's boobs

Hanging low like fruits ready
To be torn. And that's how myths
Are a woman's shackles, moistened
With saliva, never the thick milk.

Only the woman can walk on water after drowning
I've indeed spoken to broken mermaids, each to each.

The World in My Solitary Veins: Three Poems

1. SKY

Often I have described my heart
As the sky. Wiped with a washcloth.
Every picture I took during sun sets
And the red orb (Fire! Flaming!) fixing
Us with daily tasks, I've breathed slow.
Now, the breaths come even slower.
The clouds still tease. I spot shapes
The way I did as a child: Elephants
With the longest trunks ever, furry
Kittens drinking from the sky saucer,
A little girl running after a ball, and
Crocodiles in a snare. Frenzied for
Action. At times just soft strokes.
Now the shapes come even fainter.
We were taught to find colors in
the sky. Blue from airy old scars
Spread over. As though my dreams.
Until I realized dreams bled nothing
Only reality did. The way my dad's
Head bled when he had the stroke
And fell down on the wide terrace.
Often the vast screen up above
Turns into the valley of my skin
Dipping with time, tingling hard
When love's sudden cackling birds
Etched that perfect arch of a V.

Now even while the sky runs free
With no smoke prints of aeroplanes
Of our rootless journeys, I feel
There's something dripping off
Of the blankness of its pale gaze.
It is you, it says. I ask, am I?

2. WATER

Did I know
the texture of water
Before I felt it on my palm
When I rolled my days with sweat
Drops? Did I know what flutters
Each drop contained before
Dusk, before drawing curtains
Over the atrium of light?
Did I soak
my sleep with the ripples
On the horizon? Faint terraces
In the haze of summer afternoons,
Browned grass in the heist of heat
That wants water, only water.
The moment when I had dipped
My toes into a mountain river
Or when I tried seeing inside
The belly of a pond: that epiphany
Doesn't leave. Even in sorrow
And the joy of seeing an odd light
Scooping us in its fluid offering

I did not know that my own lone
World of solitude swims within
This body I inherited from decay.
A body I drink sip by sip. Molten.

3. EARTH

Truth be told, I'm tired seeing
Pictures of anointed flowers,
Well-manicured private gardens,
Common birds at uncommon hours,
And dishes dazzling like diamonds
On people's tables. I see the same
Flowers, the birds, the plates
Glittering on my curve of daily-ness.
An unsettling mirage on the senses.
I want to see the unseen: what
Of those things invisible, where
No one touched, no one was seen,
And no one spoke at all to anyone?
The face a mask, the eyes
Are probes, and the tongue
A scanner for all words unsaid.
Perhaps this earth will imprint
Itself all that on my belly, feel
The sag each muscle layer records
When we measure our own ailment,
As though recurring seismic circles.
Perhaps the summer-ridden soil
Will feel the bodies gone cold

In its wraps, while we watch
Buds flowering, unswept petals
On landscapes like heartaches.
I want to bend down and once,
Just once, touch the ground.
Perhaps it's all imagination. But
It's also to atone for the lack of touch
We've inherited. Along with it
The sudden eye for flowers, trees,
And the tedious world in mourning.

A She-Ghost Can Only Call Names

noontime. A crow perches atop the towering peepul tree, caws out
names of those dead and gone, each one. Eyes red peppers drying
in the sun, pickle jars soaking in the ruthless midday heat of rites
melting and morphing.

true, hours are slipping through the scattered sand under the
ancient
peepul. A yellow festoon flutters from a rickety cliff of a branch—
reminder of a barren wish for sons, empty blessings from
ancestors
dead, also deaf.

you know the tale of a loathsome spirit that lodges up there with
the frenetic festoon. He comes at noon, his unwilling shadowy wife
in tow and the bird—that harbinger of bad omen, stealer of
human shadows
the cacophonous crow.

nothing works. Even the sacred flag or a flashy Om on the earthen
jar
can't revive any magic, nor banish the menace. The crow watches,
screams at heretics, grows hoarse. I, the ghost bride, watch shut in
by
spirit believers. A wasted daydream.

noontime. I turn into the she-spirit, vengeful and sad. Sullen too
for being demonized. Angry at unrequited love, and I am
possessed

as she lives in me. The wary crow calls his ghoulish master, invoking
my wrath. Unstoppable wretch.

Do they see? I fly straight up on the high twig in a flash, rest my breezy
form and dangle an ungainly leg, pick on souls that dart from my stare
while the cantankerous crow can only mess up among pepper trays, jars
scaring sorry human hearts.

it's because they fear. Fear the noon's make-believe master, ruthless and swift
whose bell-jar voice haunts them in sleep. But hardly a surprise: he made a fool
of men and ghosts, demonized those that sang other prayers. Told easy lies.

Noontime. This is when I ask human vice be put at rest, perchance a fleeting
spirit takes offence. That never deters the crow from ruining our ears. It topples
pickle jars in the absolute summer heat and my reverie while calling names—
the very ones I look to scour.

from rivers and towns: fireflies and fish
conversations

those fireflies and rivers
wanted to get to the roads
over the banks of refugee shacks
over tumbling tempo hoods
over our embarrassed long and rounded vowels
just to smell the tar of dawki roads

and walk walk walk those monsoon-muddied paths
that brought us at the teetering end to ask:

will the fish wake up and recognize us?

* * *

the valley people spoke of a beautiful fish-woman
who came up to the river shore on full moon nights to taste salt
of the sands, of the tongues of pahar line cooing through tunnels
where trains ran headlong with faces hidden

they spoke of a black horse on dawn's back
a horse that munched on rising sunrays
the pasture of light
and showed them the way beyond where the magur had swum away

did you say the woman was a mermaid?

in fact, she was all fish
a woman who could swim through doors like some of us

* * *

 once through the milling crowd we had burrowed in
small change in tiny hands and counting trees of legs
we were small
we wouldn't answer strangers and princes and clowns
even though the fair with its ferris wheels had encircled us
and the crowd became the rising sea
surging in us the fear of the known
hearing hey mister acharjee babu and oh missus prerona debi

no, we aren't running away from home
once through with the milling crowd we stopped
at this lane by the strange
house that was lonely
we got home with the fair in our head
circling like afternoon pigeons while
someone screamed from afar

—come see the little girl cut in halves
come, come see her live and speak!

* * *

my uncle stuffed fireflies in his pocket
to go to the barak's banks
fireflies as baits for the fish he secretly listened to
he wooed the fish and told them stories

i'm told on gibbous nights they too
came up to tell him tales
truths and half lies
of bodies pushed under
of sad brides sleeping under waves
of fingers and rings carved on bed-mud
of money stash swaying like algae
of keys to homes that stood on one leg before falling asunder
of map etchings thrown to the fish's mouths
of words turned into sludge
of gods who wouldn't be worshipped in households

the fishing rods stretched their length
drooped in one corner of my uncle's house
they carried the load of those stories
until fireflies returned to listen to them
glittering in dark corners like children's eyes

i've seen them hum together
before the railway line outside went home
and conversations were served in coffee cups

Neurosis

I live in a lost house with four-winged rooms and a ghost cat I hate
Also, my she-shadow lives here. Unsung

Don't chide my cell phone's ring, after all, it's my full-time raga, a
wake-up call
Or my sleep meditation: Om Shantih Om

I turn on my flat-chested TV—my mailman, my unsmiling shrink,
my alter ego's voice
Friendship is not my neighbor anymore

The only humanness rises from an old bandhani rug that held your
warmth one night. Memories match your eyes, they're distant—

Remote as my cold dinner plate, like the puja thali I'd forgotten.
Thrown out petals of
Staid beliefs. Sandal paste of my sweat and all

Walking the dark corridors I fly like accidental leaves blown in by
nightly dust storms. My void and I, slipping into a stupor.

The Woman from Both Sides

When they came home they praised
Her for her naked room, the swiped floor
Kantha-stitched cushion covers and a neat
Tulsi plant doing a dhamail in the breeze
When they arrived at the garden gate they
Marveled at the roses she grew after meals
The verandah with old cane stools dozing
Before evening gods would arrive for alms
When they were asked to say a few words
They saw her brass urns glint on shelves
Filled with partition stories, re-invented,
Re-told with new metaphors washed clean
With her starched chemise in this side's sun
They wept to see her calmer than usual
So, they sat down by her body's silence
When they looked at her all wrapped in white
Sandal scents holding on tight to a gray lock
Tucked behind the right ear, they also saw
Her fingers soiled from that side, maps of tales.

Nabina Das

Ahalya's Wish

Her visit made everyone run,
fetch her special seat, water glass,
a separate special plate, later scoured
separate, after her after-work snack.
We kids ran in a tumult to see if
her teeth were different in number
than the last time, slurpy betel
juice soaked, scary monster-red.
Mother made chitchat, served her
coconut candies in summer,
black sesame sweets in winter
with jaggery or handmade bread.
Aunts poured her water slowly,
careful not to spill, not to mop
once she cleaned the outhouse,
a relic from an unknown rural life.
Once she cut the shrubs, weeded, threw
the dead skunk in a ditch and cleaned
up, we kids asked her to pick a name that
she'd like to be in her dreams so she
could be allowed to play with us,
make us clay dolls of earthly shapes.
Her dark forehead gleamed, no sindoor,
the sari-end bunched at her sagging breasts.
Her instant candor still rings in my head:
'I'd like to be made flesh, don't know the name,'
she said. 'Feet first, I will touch everything.'

Conversation

After Die Krähe (The Crow); lyrics by Wilhelm Müller. (A crow has followed him all along the way from the town. Is it waiting for him to die, so that it can eat him? It won't be long, let it keep him company to the end.)

Ravens talking in earnest is wondrous
The way they don't want to share food
And are hyperbolic about their flights
Across fallow farmlands, brown fields
Of spent ammonia, and gassy old bogs.
They have compass heads, curt motions
When they talk, ignoring the mauve sky
Of the thunder-bound clouds over a lawn.
Ravens like a drink or two with a peck
Here and there while the light dances
On their twisty heads, darkening against
A screen of sunset silk with no outlets
For ravens to fly out. So they just spar over
How many worms each of them clinched
Or how long they can keep me company
The ravens talk through my unvoiced gaze.
A familiar sight, but who'll question them
About melting as silhouettes on our eves—
Not a good thing confronting those beaks.
Ravens herald guests. So for my granny's sake
I have to wait and watch, although all I see
Them dropping from their mouth's corners
Is rotten stuff in their callous cawing prose.

The Korobi Song

Yellow our soil
Yellow the river's flow, can you see?
It brings us the faces of water—weeds
Raccoons trapped under mudslides
Yellow with silt
There was a tree in your courtyard
Lighting up the night
Yellow, some white
Finger-flowers touched by none
Yellow and yearning for a song
The Korobi sings all alone
For a Korobi who never came back home
Yellow her skin, Korobi's silk
The tree knows where the silt was sieved
Yellowing water, muddied hands
Sew limbs in the sludge, and look!
A dead rooster too.

In Perspective

Earlier it was mile-long street-corner speeches
Popcorn peppered with stinging remarks
Holding hands standing close behind the bustle
Listening to arguments as acrid as boiling oil
Partying after elders went home to sleep
Smoking, rehearsing lines for street plays
Riding a rickety bike through the outskirts of
Towns seen on TV—now cindered, broken
Lovemaking endlessly, sleeping in, sharing
News and rumors about paramilitary in town
How they called after lonely girls, after school
Clicked their guns, exhibited silly manliness
Before the cameras and boom mikes it was nice
Every one called everyone a friend, at least once
Nagaon, Baramullah, Imphal had weekend markets
Veggies, flowers, knick-knacks people loved
Before insurgency, everyone got happy and drunk
Now they have closed tea shops fearing bombs
Clothes dried in the sun before threats were heard,
No one walks or plays in those courtyards now
Newspapers quote: 'Things seemed calmer before'
And we wonder if they're still stunned like the dead.

Perhaps There's a New Sea Rising

I do this often, immerse my face in
The drifting melody of speed,
Throbbing, expecting
Pushing towards a pool of unknownness that sails slowly
Like a lost boat come home after tidal winds are dead

Leaf falls and yesteryears do
Make up some of its urgency,
Nagging, irritating fly
That snaps its sticky wings and revisits doorsteps of a house
Called memory, its driveway almost always messy

My dream hovers above meandering
Pessimism, a mountain,
Like an elephant gone to die
In peace and relative grandeur where motions kneel down
Aware that the wind takes scraps away to its bare-wall den

I wonder if then you hear songs
With birds sitting on thorns,
Bloodied to their core,
And while caravans lose paths in the swirling sea-sands
Nights pass taking stones with names inscribed and hewn

Tell me then why we need to belt
Up and buckle to our seats
For a far-flung destiny
And hold our hands when verses wither off like ink or seeds
No raccoon would eat, only this planet would dream in bits

I sieve those dreams when everything's
Gone to a dusk of rest
Beyond a highway run
Where your guns and sheep come bleating for a final kill
I'm someone with a question still slung on her breast

Perhaps there's a new sea rising
Over your brazen hand
I see its dazzle at night
Serendipity, let me weave a dream that creates boats and homes—
A web of hopefulness we wake up to in blossom-smelling lands

Nabina Das

Brutus Sings a Ruba'i

From behind, O Caesar, when I saw your trusting head
I imagined homeless folks, kids hungry in bed
Democracy raped, chasms deep all around
That noble moment let my hand, remorseless, strike you dead.

Mobocracy—a Ruba'i

This is where you took home millions
And nurtured your unworthy scions:
Those that hardly cared for a ballot to come clean
Or reach out to lambs eaten by lions!

a road not taken is a road closed to all

The atavistic life of ancient Turks or for that matter Romans, before that Scythians and who knows who else, is a testimony to the fact that human beings have, time and again, perfected the art of lying, deception and inflicting misery on others who they (or is it we) saw as 'others'.

This is so much like a road taken again and again and very much like what I read in Kay Ryan's poem last night, that a road not taken is a road closed to all, to paraphrase Ryan.
The road is here, there, everywhere. To me, it looms like blue elephants, slow and majestic. Or it also becomes dry flowers that usually fall in concentric rings from trees that hardly care.

My pets, my books, my dear ones, are all strewn along this road dusted with my little deceptions, obsessions and disharmony.

What is atavistic? What does it mean? I can't even remember now because I don't have my dictionary or my thesaurus with me. See, how I deceive myself too? I'm always taking the aid of these tools, and to a large extent, my computer—the Internet. I war on my senses, my own memory. I keep them gagged. And we as humans have been doing this over and over again until some roads— especially those that are not taken and those that want to be taken by so many—are forever closed.

War, deception, memory linger on like sticky cheese on fingers, making me sad. Sad because I wish it were different. But it also makes me happy to note that rigor is a name for everything we will write down, word by word, for charting our roads of mystery and maze.

Gandhari's Eyes

I

She had wrapped them, her eyes
so that light wouldn't invade them
and she wouldn't have
to say anything.
For words are eyes
our dilated pupils
looking at history
judging time
our words that rhyme
pal-vipal—anupal
on our tongues
red and firm like quartered tomatoes.
But surely there came a time when Gandhari grew a stare
that seared through the tatters of haze
on her eyelids' surface, the clutter
and bogs of apparent benevolence
because eyes alone guarantee
that we have spoken
to sleeping gods
and our own kinds—
she too knew.

II

Years ago while we practiced free fall
at a theater workshop, we fell
to nothingness

scripted in time
not seeing who'd catch us from behind
and uttered with sweet delicacy
elegies to souls battered,
homes looted and torn tomes
to never speak again
of a vision our eyes, our words ingrained.
Concurred.

III

Can you see now, Gandhari,
what poetry speaks? Not simply
with eyes but with a gaze
that the body donates to layers of time
after mangoes bloom, limbs
fall to the ground,
sounds of bells tell the hour
in dusty scripts that epics discard.
We can perhaps pick it
all up as we go.

Aleph

The first sound uttered is always forgotten.
Possibly it is never even a word.
Just an interjection that derives from faraway
fears or an anxious rhythm of speech.
The first sound can be heard quite clear
when groans and grunts are taken care
of with mighty sweep of authorized
hands that also stifle songs and smiles.
If you were a baby or a doddering pair
of legs, your first word would be despair
not a calligrapher's delight in dusky ink
blinking away in the heliotrope night.

In one little fable the first letter was
meant to be the first word of wonder
but no one wrote it down and so later
the ocean took it with fish and dead matter.

Narrative Limits

He was holding baby-food cartons rotten eggs ill-gotten perhaps
and soggy scraps running from a plum-dark night into what seemed
starkly bright starlight or searchlight flying with the power of bullets
in his back horse-powered from menacing police guns. He surely
said truthfully he had a starving child, but he looked like an enemy,
he did.

She was scared plumbed with interrogation, the tongue numb from
an untranslatable fear
skin shallow like swamps she jumped. Rising vapor or human crumb
her hair or breasts. Take away my hemp clothes, she pleaded, my
sentimental nesting flowers but don't take away my books, my looks
no different from you in your cities of rapturous life.

They (drove trucks, labored, choked on dust, drank spit, came
trudging here humanlike
with cherries and berries of sweat to sweeten the world, also in anger
or merriment cried,
crossed creeks, counted reluctant tax money much like you or me
and with care wiped mud from germinal faces and hands) were sent
back across the nettled fence, embattled.

They held curdled milk beans dying seeds torn clothes our discarded
marginal materials their faces like myth raked up from the bottom of
our narrative limits of scatter and filth nametag dog-leash passport
license branded on skin sizzling with fried-fish tan or tear standing
at the razor lines that distance them because of the way they walk
the streets.

Moloch

It's been long
letters did not arrive
in my name

Like time infinite
I packed lunch, tied shoelaces
set out to work

pointing to a bush
on my way, casually said,
It's a goldfinch!

Just when I eyed star fruits
in the tropical backyard
a crow ate them all

Such diligence wavers
my daily dithering
for it's been really long

Lenin (perhaps) had asked Krupskaya:
do we need kids, dear?
The Revolution is our verse

Likewise, it's been long
I haven't given birth

my verse has devoured
my own.

III

A FEW THINGS OF CONSIDERATION

Apples of Our Bodies

You can see them
Everywhere
On the body this sinuous tree
Growing
Ebbing
Whose spree for rosy ardor colors
Tastes of passion
Never grow out of fashion blooming on cheeks
Or along the creeks and valleys
Of
Breasts holding tender rotund joy
Abounding in sights that ruffle the leaves
Of our shoulders shining like moonlight
Through sieves at bent knees, jostling
Elbows

One never knows where else they grow, while
We mount them more in our
Hearts than on twigs
Lips, eyes, ample calves of splendor
Bodies small and big all gravitating
Towards the sepia soil of
Rest
Where at seasons' behest one day
They'll lie
Limb by limb, core by core, before they
Die telling
Autumn tales, sweetening the earth's sore.

A Few Things of Consideration

'If we choose, we can live in a world of comforting illusion.' —Noam Chomsky

This a far-off place where I am lodged
between news nights, a foggy web, shores
of dawning illusion after the day's rowing
is done. Am a chalice half-full, half-seen.

This face is me, although another continent
brown and mysterious earth, I tell all friends
while they are nodding to the lullabies of globalization,
reading and debating Stiglitz ad nauseum
desiccated words that drink churned hopes.

Therefore, this has to be a mind that swims
I have concurred, where waking lies under
a Delhi sun or a New York cloud ever so
languid from gaping at gregarious billboards:
Pepsi, Nike and maximum mantras after a
game of duck and hide daily on our wobbly
sides as I can see: it is her neck, his body that
winces quite like mine cries from battles and
for beans, in sincere scare and loathing, searches
a reason to love and call everything by impermanent
names; for example: I am, or, we are.

A Soothsayer's Dilemma

When she said prophecies make the sky spin like a roulette table,
she meant while taking
chances, they reach the end of palpability, each courting a few
unexplored desires.

She said prophecies would let their winding hands circle my fleshy
roots, digging amply inside Apollo's oracles, welcoming a change
in spring's sparkled honeyed light.

I asked if Future is a scene, a fête where men and women bestow
abhaya; laugh. Because
They're shown grand, animated, in prints of red and sepia tones in
books of prophecies.

She said because we can't read the future we melt inside our tacky
floors hopelessly shelled
with sleep's call. But they still come, the prophecies, like soft
footfalls and infantile taps.

My mother's disbelief, when I said prophecies invade my bark
before turning into the ark
when new rivers, depths unknown, are created, seemed like a
verse. Prophetic overtures.

Nabina Das

Genesis Trilogy

I. What the Serpent Said to Her

You may follow me towards
A destiny of multitude
As I draw it
On the sand
In a tailspin

You may think I'm a green bough
And my eyes buds
Of a spring
That'll not scorn you
Because you have bones
Shaped like a bow or harp
That shoots or sings

We can celebrate your footfalls
Give them the name of a music.

If you follow me.

II. What She Said to Us

These songs are not mine
Nor these epic stories
These rivers
Were dug elsewhere
No wonder the water's gone brackish

This fiber is too coarse
For my bark and soul
This food does not nourish
These walls were built
For your cattle
Not me.

Don't tilt your weights
Don't strike your rib so hard
If you don't
I will tell you if
Cloud-walking is a virtue
And if, my talking, my waking, with you
Is a virtue you can hold on to
Like my arms.

III. What the Poet Thought

What came out during a
revelation on the state of the man
Is that He lacked wings
Though hundreds of years had passed and
He Never even bothered to be like Icarus
That mythical moron
The unfortunate but imaginative one
Who took a plunge for things most loved.

Besides, what She recounted,
He had already lost in his dreamless

sleeps the language of liturgy
Forgotten in His worships.

Like She was forgotten to
Him like leaves rustled
unheard
Like serpents laying their calm heads down,
seeking to warm their skin were not seen as bards.

I, only I was left to sing.

Tunes from a Migrant's Song

There is a land
of not-plenty I come from

And another where milk flows

Like tiny flies on garbage
rotting in numerous strands

I close-fist my hand and watch the
veins for this is blood for giving and spending

In new fields and
farms till crows fly
away home

She gives food and dollar bills
and the meadows roll into

Spicy treats
my tongue welcomes like the dandelions of spring

No papers and fewer fears
of the unknown, I am delivered and my
soul to a bandage-unwrapped hand
blessing the spirit that brought me

Away, far away from boot kicks,
sidewalk pleas, homes that never knew roofs.

Nabina Das

Another Evening

When they brought back their
street carts of rainbow fare, they
talked
in an even tone—one joked,
the other swore merrily. Both sprinkled
water on the dusty street corner at the busy
market, set up little plastic dolls, cheap
household stuff, and a pile of
scarves, also T-shirts that say: *I love
NY! Viva Che!* They told me they
had started this day with prayers and
flowers inside placid empty rooms or
in front
of tiny gods who smiled
while they both wept to
think of the day they didn't
die.
Two years is a geological
time span of dust and dirt
mingling. Exactly after the
horrible event when cars
burst and cycles tore but
because folks read about it
long ago in newspapers
it was odd to see them both
wipe their eyes with collars
sooty black. Was it a blessing
to be back?

To be in the place where memories
rot? One said he was having trouble
without his wife, an empty home.
The other repeated with sighs
how he
never found on this spot his teenaged
son. It was the same street corner,
where they had settled down again
with their day's job, enticing
adamant kids and reluctant
parents
to buy, from their friendly rainbow
fare, even if folks didn't care much for
a plastic comb, balloons from their
carts, pipe-horns, sunny hair clips,
sundry things. This is the only prayer
now they sing
that they didn't die from that evening's blast
but returned like moss over gray stones
after rains washed blood from wounds and sighs of loss.

Nabina Das

The Death Row Inmate Sings a Ruba'i

A night that held my hand and promised a day
to you, to field flowers and the sunshine of May,
is witness to my vice or folly uncommitted.
So, take this last letter and put it away.

Border Votes

We came across the paddy fields at dawn
Shall we then go back at night to emerge
The next day and stain our fingers with ink?
We can bring stale rice soaked in lime juice

To keep us going, paddy field to
macadam
Counting tidy sums that are yours; ours
too
In sickness and hunger, bribing or
buying
So that across another fence of
otherness
We stand defenseless, watch this
business
Of men and women calling us their
kind
And then looking away at ballot
stamps
To erase our hands, holds; stump our
faces.

Lost Landscape

Bamboo flutes
that my father had played
once the leather-jacketed
book
that had always been a prop on my
table the borgeet from the Namghar
in sticky caramel noons
my teacher's voice across the
blackboard that death silenced and
my mother's rosebushes of hope.
What remains when blue hills
weep or the red river goes into
hiding?
Even the goddess watches from the
hilltop squirming at slow blood oozing
from deep coves of deathliness that
Neelachal never for once has known.
What dies when new words are
born? Not the wounds, not the
burning shame. I wonder if I still
should paint
those paddy fields, peacocks and
skies with my brush of golden taint.

When Langston Hughes Visited My Home

The name was strange and the
book was shiny dark
Thin, freckled jacket, like my
angry pre-teen face
on the table

The title kept calling in a
jingle-jangle Assamese
refrain I kept saying it out
loud:
'Hey Xurjo Uthi Aha'!

Why it exhorted the sun to
rise, accept the challenge of
a new dream that flamed
brighter and purer
And why the smaller typeface said:
poems by dark-limbed poets, a
collection, I had no idea then

Dark limbs were not
seen on our book
covers
only limbs were,
then Krishna is just not
a word for a god, it
dawned on me, but skins
and cheeks and strong

arms of poetic force on
my table

Also the end of crowing
nights when a poet came
home inside the covers of a
book, smiling: That day is
past!

It's Showtime Now

You mustn't worry whether the
weather Is fine or muggy in our cities
these days We'll be inside the box,
special seats The Stateroom all to
ourselves, we can Sing in abandon in
Jacques Brel's voice No wonder I
hear people discuss Le Gaz
And this all when we can all have fun in
a Bunch, say yay to Hercule Yakko
while Crowding above our pothole of
jibes and Cramming into neighbors'
shoes spilling Ammonia with love, only
love, but wait! Will someone say we
wanted to spoil the Fun? No, not when
we sing and chant: Take Me Out To the
Ballgame! The rest will Follow your
imagination, call it chaos or Disdain,
it's never too crowded to catch a sham.

Writing Vaudeville

Because the days of
dreaming and imagination are so much a part
of the way we construct our existence, the way we
pay taxes, sign certificates to say
we haven't cheated
or maybe have, our
lives in a way,
became one of
revelation, Vaudeville, polite!

'After you folks finish
shopping in the box-stores, gulping Dr. Peppers
and belching out your frozen-at-birth-warmed
bacon-filled tacos…'
I asked this of all
that I passed by as a
last try

(I have a trained dog
fetching my acidity
pills miracle elixir
bottles
    big-time billowing
            bills).
   So, emboldened, I
          asked.
'Can you lead me to the eyes of the
beast?' 'The eyes!' Retorted the portly

man who sits daily by
Lost Tribe Café.
'Asking a blind man
about
Finding the beast's eyes
takes some nerve!' He
muttered.
I stepped out gloom-
wrapped in low autumn's
vagaries.
'When you don't see with eyes,
you start living with stuff around,
the things around you, not
in front of them, did you
know?' A woman from the
café
emerged mournful yet mellow.
'Forgive my old man, he's a Paul Cox fan,
watched his flicks when he had eyes, good
ones.'
Motionless she stood, hands on
her old man's shoulders—a faded Pieta
on a renovated worship house shelf.

Newsroom Novena

Furry friends, a flamingo forest and a frosty treat
Begging for dough, zapping depression and musical
condoms. Chained to the radiator? For our own good, dear
reader! Coveted, French and now in the super malls in
your town. Find a life filled to the brim with still more to
add.
Dice-K on the gyroball, Dow averaged and more and
more… Goofball, Office salesman living a city dream, not
me!
But a date with destiny on the 7th of July (oh, it's just a date).
Hitting the road for some hot-man-on-bike action, you bet.
Meanwhile, Wallace and Gromit spearhead citizens' project
And felons are allowed to work at school for the deaf and
blind.

The setting is a gay bathhouse in the mid-1970s, you knew.
Is that an actress wearing her uterus on the sleeve?
Is that you?
It's a novena spending time with sound
byte inside heads.

In-road

Afternoon in the city. Heat falls. The roads are on a boil.
The shantytown people are straining lentils in the drain.
Roads, will you please step aside a bit and let us rest?
Roads, why is it so that you're in the habit of moving always?
Roads, you are dipping toes into the melted tar, how long?

Afternoon makes hearts crisper than fries, upackaged.
The city is a mannequin yawning at the sky. Clouds stream.
Onlookers are swarming up fast on the veins of the roads.
Forms move, feet shuffle, breaths drop, all in tandem.
I'm adjusting my sunshade and speaking into the mobile.
I ignore the pigeons' gurgle and shit from store awnings
and still say: Roads, will you take me to that only love?
Roads, take me barefoot, take me on a swing, take me
from my navel through my spine, from roads to roads.

Nabina Das

Living Room Homily

Women talking in high voices
Tingling streets
An indolent afternoon in the library
—All that glides up to whisper:
How we love life

After poems are read
Blood is spilled
Bee stings are removed
From unresponsive arms

We can measure up to reality
As though it's a challenge
We can read minds
As though it's an ancient art, revived

Furry dogs bustling
Smothering fleur du soir
A fleeting glance after remembrance
—Nothing that stops enchantment,
To say we love life

After you come back home
Hobble in the pantry
After newsprint withers
Becomes compost in the bin

I can clamor under the bright light
Straighten my pleats and scarf
I can wake up before dawn
As though night never came.

When identity and epistemology hit one hard

Do you remember those filmmakers we'd met at their St. Michel home
by the tired Seine staring away from the tourists? Their walls full of wild masks
and *objets d'art* from Morocco, Tunis or wherever. Pretty much like an antique farm
or a museum of exotic delights. Yes, I'm talking about *that* conversation, *that* climb
UP the civilizational ladder as I'd nodded absentmindedly over lunch, eyeing a shy rain
on the French window. I even dropped a slippery asparagus on my plate, damn!

It all started from them saying how the magnificent windows can't be opened, damn
those foreigners that crawl every brick of the posh locale! For outsiders even homes,
people's homes, are some sort of a pop-a-penny show, and yadi yadi yada. The rain
was falling pretty hard then, unseasonal. Our friends hated it too. They said the rare masks—
one was from Ararat—suffered from damp walls soaking their surfaces. Who's gonna climb
that hill (beyond modernity's scope) again, go up, just for art's sake, to a smelly goat farm?

I saw their point, so strongly made. For avant-garde artists who've been farming
their skills worldwide and for those that have read Voltaire in all his damning
alacrity about humankind, you'd agree, we were relatively new climbers

on philosophy's totem pole. Still, something the ethno-movie makers said hit home.
I mean, made me forget the right ways to eat asparagus and sit up. I'm sure to have masked
my surprise, for it's all *bonnes manières*. But hey, it's also my 'cultural' upbringing to rain

questions on any artistic claim (no getting away from the prototype, you see!). The rain
muted our discussion but then YOU asked politely (gosh, so typical of Ivy League-farmed
scholars), 'Does she really, really remind you of *that*? Although true, we all wear identity masks
that we ourselves love, or get dumped upon.' (Kicking me under the table: 'Quiet, you.') Damn
your sensitivity! Just to assure I'm no believer in *idée fixe*, I again rallied my sentences home:
'It's actually funny to hear I look like a Mexican or one of those folks who regularly climb

over the fences to live or die their American Dream. No, wait, not funny. I do enjoy climbing,
backs and stairs and hills and walls and fences—perhaps not trees—come snow, shine or rain!
And no climb gets better, more meaningful, if one's looking for a home away from home:
a little house, green lawn, plastic deer grazing (the prize from cherry-picking in the farms).
The erudite filmmakers nodded: '*Mais oui.*' 'But no one offered me a job in Paris, damn!'
I joked. They looked thoughtful. You rolled your eyes. But I knew our friends wore no masks

when they sincerely said they could try (not for me) ask an acquaintance who's a damask
dealer somewhere on the un-glitzy right bank or near the rough Pigalle where tourists climb
the hill to see the city. Our friends did know a few un-papered folks, only if those damned
people would take such jobs. This was such a humanitarian concern, and raining
sympathies on have-nots 'doesn't always help'. We asked, why! 'Oh, *imaginez*, cheese-farming,
yeah, camembert! And vinification, the *Beaujolais* too, gone to them! France is now their home.'

We walked out later, masked in the summery St. Michel rain;
climbed the bridge from where Algerians were once pushed off to die, farming
damned histories in our heads. You said, 'Curry *pâté* this evening!' We headed home.

The Rhyme of an Obituary Writer
OR
Death of a Poet

I have a new job. I'm no longer
a poet. I have a new pen. And
I no longer know how to rhyme.
They call me an obit-writer. An
oracle at the tip of my pen for all
who need a makeover. I write
about powerful men who led to
kill. I call them poets. I'm an obit-
writer for hardliner women. I call
them beautiful names: Mother,
saint, leader, nurturer. I so love
my new job as an obit-writer. I
set aside all carnage, pogroms,
grafts, cover-ups, blood-letting.
All Rathyatras, demolitions, heists,
and clamping down on rights.
My new pen writes about men
and women the nation wants to
worship in frenzied newsrooms.
Their suave name-studded suits,
their plucky Kanjeevaram pleats.
This also brings me to say that I
shall be an obit-writer for more
folks in future. They'll hire me
for the swift flourish of my pen.

I'll be writing about that loud man
who will never hear out others.
I'll call him a singing nightingale.
For the man who made it easy
for all lies to be normalized, I
will call him a soothsayer of times.
For the killer whose hands still
stink, my pen will make him a king
of hearts. For the seller of forests
the obit will propose we award
her a green crusader badge. I
definitely am not a poet any longer.
My pen doesn't like any anger
or even love. They want to send
love to the death cell, call it jihad.
I'll be sitting in a corner all day
writing about a world of crooks,
slowly weave stories for a book
where the dead who sang, spoke
up, loved, and yearned for freedom
will vanish. My pen will not dream.
Today I'm an obit-writer, no poet.

Vanaprastha in the New Millennium

Lenin's angular profile studies the ceiling's corner
Raised stiff, suitably elegant and intellectual
Photo-framed on the freedom-sky-blue wall

Lacquer bowls, Russian, with puckered faces not
Able to see their own paint-smeared smooth bellies
In a melee of scores of seashells nestling in them
Short changes from long-ago family holidays

An office union calendar, don't know who got it
Hangs urgent and fluttery in the semi-spring breeze
Mondays, Sundays, paydays, all days organized well
As in a spreadsheet, boxy dates to enable scribbles
About meetings, reviews and occasional lockouts

My parents did not have the heart to change the TV
The color tube's a bit busted, spills green more
But the screen beams in Nat Geo & History they watch
In a silent slump from re-painted couches of Assam cane

The brass xorai is not for praying. 'True is it, your dad's a
Red?' A neighborhood uncle had asked me, 'doesn't pray.'
Do I know? I also know Dad waited with us for prasad
From Mom's puja evenings of camphor, Lakshmi's calm

That's her favorite chair, those his books, cobweb
Under curtains long unwashed, my embroidered
Dancers, brother's rickety racket, the portly phone
Awaiting the ring of our brawls. Where will it all go?

We all laughed, sang, ate and told each other stories here
One of those about this house of memories now on sale.

Six-Mile Creek

Sleep is a sharp river bend
Geology too, on a face-smooth rock
One that climbs up the banks
From the creek that flows
Behind my hill on a cascading street
Called water, silent at night
They say the trout should
Flock after this neon winter passes
And now only sprigs float
Below the dam after six miles
Where half-nude youngsters jump into
The liquidy sheet ignoring signs
That say 'don't'. They still do
With their sudden laughter waking up
Us who sleep on the rocky shore.

Nabina Das

Morphologia

My mother's litheness has melted
on to a lump of thin muscles limp
her skin a silken furrowed Kabuki fan
she's not plump anymore, my Ma
those breasts once like mountained pies
now they whisper each other stories
of passion that hangs loose, peeled
her mouth's cinnamon is browned
and her hair more jasmine than kohl
the white roses at the porch know
have seen the bloom fade, with years' trim
and she worships more her favorite
man-god, feeds him like an infant
now that she can't have us on her lap anymore

*   *

Seeing distant rivers on the TV she starts
off about the playground by the Surma
and the tea gardens where jhumur
was the first step she had learned

*   *

My mother's city was not her friend, she
loved it only from the Xarania's top
by its aloof white dome, her brown eyes
mapping the Moha-baahu's breadth
for a lore she sung us from her past

*   *

Now afternoons pass, evenings flower
with incense in their hearts, she lies
from the long day of her godhuli life
bundled and river-clay-soft on her bed
as if no bones or flesh make that body
it makes me utter in a nervous even tone:
'Ma, will you wake up ... shall I get you some tea?'

Vector

It is never a mean feat to catch a light
Light that is bright and essentially a ray
From a source that stays alive through time
Although we tally time into days and nights

Some have called it a hopeful disposition
Others have derided it all the same
Seeing how passionate some of us are about
Catching warm light from ethereal heights

But fireflies have done it now and then
After balmy rains on empty mountain paths
Unafraid of sudden gusts through shrubs
Only since they followed a source awakened

So, my hands are carriers, sometimes red
Or egg-yellow masses of the declining sun
They fumble inside coat pockets to find time
For catching light whenever it is aground.

ABOUT THE POET

Nabina Das is a poet and writer based in Hyderabad. She is the author of three poetry collections—*Sanskarnama, Into the Migrant City,* and *Blue Vessel*—a novel titled *Footprints in the Bajra,* and a short fiction volume titled *The House of Twining Roses: Stories of the Mapped and the Unmapped.* Nabina's first book of translations *Arise out of the Lock: 50 Bangladeshi Women Poets in English* appeared in early 2022. A Rutgers-Camden MFA alumna, Nabina is the editor of *Witness: The Red River Book of Poetry of Dissent,* and co-editor of *40 under 40, an Anthology of Post-globalisation Poetry.*

Nabina is a 2017 Sahapedia-UNESCO fellow, a 2012 Charles Wallace Creative Writing alumna (Stirling University, Scotland), and a 2016 Commonwealth Writers features correspondent. Her poems appear in *Poetry* (Poetry Foundation), *Prairie Schooner, The Caravan, The Indian Quarterly,* and *Economic and Political Weekly,* among several others.

Nabina has worked most recently as a teaching faculty, a journalist for 10 years, and also as a media executive in NGOs and industry bodies in the area of Gender, Development, Child Welfare, and the Environment.